DOUBLETALK

By the same Author:

Cages (*Snowangel* and *Epiphany*)
Telemachus Clay — A Collage for Voices
Doubletalk (*The Dirty Old Man* and *Sarah and The Sax*)

DOUBLETALK

Lewis John Carlino

Random House · New York

DOUBLETALK *was first presented by Cheryl Crawford and Roger L. Stevens at the Theatre de Lys, New York City, on May 4, 1964, with the following cast:*

The Dirty Old Man

THE OLD MAN	Franchot Tone
MARY	Amy Taubin
CHUCK	Gregory Rozakis

Sarah and The Sax

SARAH	Ruth White
THE SAX	Clarence Williams III

Directed by Cyril Simon

Design and Lighting by Boyd Dumrose

Costumes by Julia Lusk

Musical Score by Al Cohn

The Dirty Old Man

To Maria, for all the things unspoken

A promontory overlooking a stretch of deserted coast in northern California. It is fall. The grasses are burnt brown and golden, creating sharp contrast against the green of Torrey and Monterrey Pines that grow almost horizontally because of the constant push of wind.

As the curtain opens, it is late afternoon, and the sun has begun to cast its early pinks and ambers on everything so that all seems to pulsate with a fire of its own. It is one of those moments in nature when the harmonies of light and color and sound fix and suspend themselves to reveal the secrets of its nexus. There is a long moment of silence, then we hear twigs breaking and the sound of heavy breathing coming from the thicket upstage left. An OLD MAN *emerges from the tangle of shrubs and walks to stage center. He is breathing hard from a long climb. He wears an old and tattered sweatshirt and a scarf around his neck; he carries a paper bag and a pint of Chianti. His face is browned from endless hours in the sun. There are two things one notices immediately about this man: his eyes and his hands. His eyes are young and move quickly, with a sort of hunger, devouring each leaf, each tree and wave with a determined urgency. They are the kind of eyes that reveal the man behind the face, the prism through which a soul focuses on the world. His hands are small and delicate. In all they do, they move with careful and deliberate movements. In all they touch, they seem to linger, as if to try to hold fast the memory of textures, weights, and temperatures. The* OLD MAN, *still breathing heavily, walks down-*

stage. Then, on second thought, he turns and walks back to the edge of the thicket. He parts it and yells.

OLD MAN   Damn you, hill! You think you can beat me? Not yet, damn you! Thought you had me that time. Ha, ha! I spit on you. (*He spits*) What do you think of that? (*He nods, grunting, and walks back to center stage. He reaches inside his shirt, rubbing his chest*) Come on, come on, you stupid heart. Stop that! You want the hill to know what it's doing to us? (*He winces with pain*) Stop it! (*His breath comes easier*) There. That's better. That'a boy. Good. I don't know why I put up with such foolishness. (*He looks up at the scene before him. He smiles and salutes*) Good afternoon, ocean. Good afternoon, beach, sky. Good afternoon, phylum *Colenterata,* phylum *Curipedia, Brachyura.* (*He turns and salutes the trees*) And you, gentlemen; *Sequoiadendron, Pinus.* (*He takes the bottle of wine and places it carefully on the rock near him. From the paper bag he takes small pieces of salami, cheese, and bread. The cheese and salami he puts into opposite ends of his left fist. He holds the bread in his right hand. He is about to eat when he remembers something. He takes out a small pocket knife, cuts small portions of cheese, bread, and salami, and scatters them on the ground. He uncorks the bottle of wine and pours a small amount. He nods to himself, smiling. He looks up at the sky*) That's for the gods. (*He begins to eat, alternating cheese and salami by turning his fist one way, then the other, Italian style. He takes a sip of wine and smiles. All is well with the world*) Ah, good. Very good. Eh, stomach, what do you think? (*He takes a long drink of wine. He*

6

looks at the bottle) Twinkle, twinkle, little grape, how
you do incite to rape. (*He grows angry with himself.
This becomes a sort of conversation with his conscience
as he eats*) Shut up, fool! Forgive me. My incipient
senility. *That's no excuse!* Right! One must think mor-
ally no matter what one thinks. *You're an imbecile!* I
thought you realized that already. *Don't talk back!* I'm
sorry. *You certainly are!* There's no need for sarcasm.
I've apologized. *You're always apologizing. You think
that solves everything? Well, it doesn't. All these
thoughts about rape and girls and the rest. It's disgusting
at your age.* I won't repeat the grape-rape verse ever
again. *Promise?* Yes. *Then I accept your apology. You
have to do something about these lecherous outbursts.*
I'll try. *Good.* You have no sense of humor. *There's work
to do. Notebook?* Here. (*He takes a small notebook and
pencil from his pocket*) *Pencil?* Yes. *Begin.* Yes. (*He
studies the scene before him. He takes a drink of wine
and begins to write*) Now let's see . . . Today, the water
is metal-green. The same green of those fat midsummer
flies. It seems to have the viscosity of oil. (*He takes a
drink of wine*) Yes, the water is thick today. The sky
arranges itself in strata of purple, indigo, vermilion, and
just at the surface of the water, mauve. Oh, yes, that's
good. I wonder if mauve is right? Perhaps too much
blue . . . No, it's right. (*He sniffs the air*) The air today
is filled with insinuations. The most noticeable insinuators seem to be the scrub oaks. (*He sniffs again*) Their
contribution, a sort of acrid musk. (*He reads what he
has written*) Insinuators . . . No, that's too rhetorical.
. . . most noticeable *scent*, the scrub oaks. That's better.
Simple and clear, simple and clear. Yes, my dear, be of

7

cheer, never fear, try not to leer, lend an ear, let's have a beer. (*He drinks*) Twinkle, twinkle, little grape, how you do incite to rape. (*He laughs*) *You promised!* Right. I'm sorry. *Lecher!* I said I was sorry. *Get on with it!* Yes. (*He goes back to his notebook*) The next scent is cedar, then the pines (*He sniffs*), lungwort, sea lavender, kale, and . . . and kidneys . . . kidneys. *Kidneys!* Damn you! (*He holds the bottle of wine up*) There was a time when you could hold two of these before I had to help you out. You have no appreciation for good vintage. This is Ruffino fifty-nine. Ach, what's the use? You both are a great disappointment.

(*He puts the bottle on the ground and walks off into the thicket, unbuttoning his fly. A moment passes. We hear movement in the thicket, stage right.* CHUCK *and* MARY *enter. They are both about sixteen.* CHUCK *carries a blanket and a quart bottle of beer.* MARY *carries a transistor radio from which we hear some soft music. She looks around in apprehension*)

CHUCK   This is ok here.
(*He spreads the blanket*)

MARY   Maybe there's a spot a little further.
(*She begins to move stage right.* CHUCK *sits on the blanket and takes a drink*)

CHUCK   This is *all right*. We've changed twice already. Now come on. What's the matter, now?

MARY   Nothing.

8

CHUCK Then what'a you acting like that for? Here.
(*He hands her the bottle. She takes it, drinks, and
hands it back. She looks at the ocean.* CHUCK *waits
impatiently*)

MARY Oh, gee, Chuck, ain't it beautiful? Look at all the
colors.

CHUCK We didn't come to look at the view.

MARY I know, I know. You don't have to tell me.

CHUCK Then come on.

MARY What if anybody should come?

CHUCK Up here? Are you kidding?

MARY Well, just suppose?

CHUCK Look, are you gonna, or are you not gonna? If
you're not, we'll go back. Now make up your mind.

MARY Ok, ok! Don't get mad. You don't have to get mad,
do you?

CHUCK What'a you think, you're a big deal or something?
You're no big deal, so stop coming off like Orphan Annie.

MARY All *right!* I said I would, didn't I? (*Pause*) I know
you wanted Linda instead of me.

CHUCK Yeah, yeah.

MARY I couldn't help it if I got your number.

CHUCK Oh, man. (*He drinks*) Look, no talk, just action. You understand? Action!

MARY Ok.
(*She takes her sweater off*)

CHUCK An' change that station. (*He changes the station to some fast jazz*) That's better.
(MARY *starts to unbutton her blouse. The* OLD MAN *steps out from the bushes as surprised as they*)

OLD MAN Oh, excuse me.

CHUCK (*Getting up*) Hey, Hey, Hey, what is this?

OLD MAN I'm sorry . . .

MARY (*Fumbling to get her sweater back on*) See? I told you.
(*She turns off the radio*)

CHUCK What's with you, pops?

OLD MAN I don't understand.

CHUCK What're you doing here?

OLD MAN I could ask you the same question if it wasn't so obvious.

CHUCK (*Grabbing him by the shirt*) What're you, a wise guy?

MARY Chuck!

CHUCK Followin' us ta get a little peek, huh?

OLD MAN No.

CHUCK *Sure* you were!

OLD MAN No. I was here before you. I just answered a call of nature, came back, and here you were.

CHUCK Don't give me that.

MARY Chuck, it doesn't matter. Let's . . .

CHUCK Will you shut up and just let me handle this?

OLD MAN He's right, young lady. You should let him handle it.

CHUCK Who asked for your two cents?

OLD MAN Look, I can prove I was here. (*He goes to wine bottle, which has been partially obscured by a bush. He holds it up*) These are mine. I live here. I mean there (*He points*), at the bottom of the hill, on the beach. I come here every afternoon.

CHUCK Yeah, well you're rained out today, pops. Beat it.

OLD MAN Oh, I couldn't do that. Look at that sky. Already the hue and chroma are changing. See how the indigo and vermilion are . . . (*He jots in his notebook*) Oh, I couldn't do that. I'd miss the whole thing.

CHUCK (*To* MARY) You hear that? He's some kind of crazy geek.

MARY We can find another place.

CHUCK No. *No!* We're not moving. Let *him* find another place. Ok, pops, I told you to cut out.

OLD MAN I'm sorry.
          (*He sits and writes.* CHUCK *looks around, spots a stick, picks it up and approaches the* OLD MAN)

MARY Chuck!

CHUCK Look, geek, I asked you nice. Now are you gonna get out of here or not?
          (*The* OLD MAN *continues writing.* CHUCK *raises the stick to strike.* MARY *runs behind him and grabs it*)

MARY Don't! He's an old man.

OLD MAN (*At his notebook*) An ignominious defense.

CHUCK Let go!

MARY We'll find another place. Please.

CHUCK Let go, I said!

(He pulls the stick away from her, and raises it to strike)

MARY   Don't!
(She covers her face with her hands. The OLD MAN *turns and looks at* CHUCK, *and there is something in his face, his age, a look of pitiful fear, that stops him from striking.* CHUCK *drops the stick and turns angrily to* MARY)

CHUCK   Sure, you wanna look for another place so you can go on playing games. I got the picture. Well, baby, you just aced yourself out of the Goddesses. All mouth and no action, that's you. Well, I'm cuttin' out. An' you know what? I'm leaving you here with the geek. Make out with him. He's about your speed.

MARY   I'll *do* it. I *swear* I will!

CHUCK   I wouldn't have you on a bet, now. You wanna be a big deal, be one. But not with me. I don't know why they ever nominated you, anyway. You're stupid. You're just a big, square, stupid raunch. Get away from me.

MARY   Chuck?
(She rushes to him and grabs his arm)

CHUCK   Get *away!* I'm not *kidding!* Have a ball.
(He pushes her away and exits upstage. MARY *puts her face in her hands and cries. The* OLD MAN *glances at her and continues jotting.* MARY's *crying*

finally diminishes to a sniffle. She turns off the radio, angrily. The OLD MAN *turns to her)*

OLD MAN   Don't you have a handkerchief?

MARY   No. Shut up!

OLD MAN (*Holding out his handkerchief to her*)   Here.

MARY (*Wipes her nose on her sleeve*)   I don't want anything from you. You've ruined it. You've ruined *everything!*

OLD MAN   Maybe your boyfriend will come back.

MARY   He won't! And he's not my boyfriend. He's a God.

OLD MAN   Really? Which one—Mars?

MARY   Ha, ha, you're laughing now, but you weren't a minute ago. You were scared, weren't you? Chuck doesn't take any jazz from anybody. See the way he grabbed that stick? He could've killed you if it wasn't for me.

OLD MAN   Yes, I think so. Thank you.

MARY   Skip it.

OLD MAN   Ok.

MARY   Now, what the hell am I going to do?

OLD MAN   He'll come back.

MARY   What'a you know? He won't!

OLD MAN   Why not?

MARY   Because he's a God! What'sa matter, you stupid or something?

OLD MAN   I guess I am.

MARY   Ain't you never heard of the Gods and Goddesses of Hamilton High?

OLD MAN   No, I haven't.

MARY   Hey, you *are* a ding-a-ling. Where you been, mister, in orbit?

OLD MAN   Well, you see, I'm sort of isolated out here.

MARY   You *must* be! (*A long pause. She walks and looks off, down at the beach*) You really live down there?

OLD MAN   Yes.

MARY   By yourself?

OLD MAN   Yes.

MARY   Like a hermit or something like that?

OLD MAN   I guess you might call me that.

MARY   Jeeze, what a creepy way to live. Hey, you got any cigarettes?

OLD MAN   I don't smoke. I'm sorry.
(*He takes a drink of wine*)

MARY   Oh, great! I'm stranded in the middle of nowhere with some old wino and I ain't even got cigarettes!
(*The* OLD MAN *lowers the bottle from his lips. He has been hurt.* MARY *sees his expression. There is a long silence. The* OLD MAN *sighs and goes back to his notebook, speaking as he writes*)

OLD MAN   How do you like being a Goddess?

MARY   I'm *not* one. You fixed that.

OLD MAN (*Looking at her*)   I did?

MARY   Oh yeah, you fixed it fine.

OLD MAN   How?

MARY   Skip it. It doesn't matter now, anyway.

OLD MAN   I'd like to know.

MARY   I bet you would.

OLD MAN   You can't blame me for something and then not tell me what it is.

MARY   Ok, you wanna know, mister? Chuck was my initiation number. When you're nominated to the Goddesses, you get an initiation number that's one of the Gods. Chuck was my number and I had to *do* it with him to become a Goddess. Ok, so you were here and you wouldn't move so that's what I'm blaming you for. Ok, so let's just forget about it.

OLD MAN He isn't your boyfriend?

MARY I didn't even know him before today.

OLD MAN All the Goddesses get the same initiation?

MARY Sure. Why?

OLD MAN (*Clearing his throat*) Oh, no reason. Just curious.

MARY (*Another silence*) Well, anyway, I'll see you. (*She starts to leave*)

OLD MAN How will you get back?

MARY Dunno. Hitch a ride down on the highway.

OLD MAN That's dangerous.

MARY I can take care of myself.

OLD MAN Sure. I'll tell you what. I'll make you a five-dollar bet Chuck comes back within an hour.

MARY Are you kidding?

OLD MAN (*Takes out a bill and waves it*) Here it is.

MARY   What a set-up. Too bad I don't have five bucks.

OLD MAN   I'll accept your radio as collateral.

MARY   You're just throwin' that away. He won't come.

OLD MAN   It's easy money if you're so sure. If he's not back within an hour, it's yours. (*He looks at his watch*) It's four thirty-five. We got a bet?

MARY   You're not kidding, now?

OLD MAN   I never kid about money. Especially mine. Ok?

MARY (*Shrugs*)   Ok. Boy, you're something else. I mean something else.

OLD MAN   What?

MARY   I don't know. (*She walks around with her arms behind her head*) Oh boy, look'a me. I'm stranded in the desert with an old wino and no cigarettes.

OLD MAN   This is not the desert, it's the beach. I'm sorry about the cigarettes, and I'm not a wino.
    (*He takes a drink*)

MARY (*Indicating his bottle*)   Yeah, what's in there, Ovaltine?

OLD MAN   The consumption of wine is no proof of debauchery.

MARY   You sound like one of my teachers with all those words like that. Hey, were you ever a teacher?

OLD MAN   Never.

MARY   You sure sound like one.

OLD MAN   Sorry to disappoint you.
(*He writes in his notebook*)

MARY   Are you kidding? I hate teachers.

OLD MAN   Hate is a strong word.

MARY   It's true. Think they know it all. Like Mr. Comi. "Wales has a population of 2,489,600 and is 8016 square miles." Who cares? What difference does it make? You care if Wales is 8016 square miles?

OLD MAN (*Smiling*)   Not particularly.

MARY   See? That's what I mean. Think they're smart. You can't even read a comic in study hall any more. Dirty cop-outs.

OLD MAN   I think you're being unfair.

MARY   Yeah, you would.
(*She watches him*)

OLD MAN   What's your name?

MARY   Mary.

OLD MAN   That's very nice.

MARY   It stinks. It's gooky, rinky-tink. I mean who the hell you know is named Mary? Mary, Mary, quite contrary. It's like a nursery rhyme.

OLD MAN (*Still writing*)   Well, let's see. There was Mary Magdalene.

MARY   Who's that?

OLD MAN   She was a woman of easy virtue who lived in Biblical days.

MARY   You mean a hustler?

OLD MAN   You know about hustlers?

MARY   Hey, what'a you think I'm some kind of Mongolian idiot or something?

OLD MAN   Not at all.

MARY   You know how many houses we got in Hamilton? Eight. An' boy, you should see the action when the Cholos come up ta dig potatoes. I mean, it's like Disneyland. You ever been to Disneyland?

OLD MAN   No.

MARY   Boy, that's something else. I mean really something else. So who else you know by the name of Mary?

OLD MAN   Well, the mother of Jesus Christ was named Mary.

MARY   You mean God?

OLD MAN   Some people call him that.

MARY   Hey, you really believe in that? You know, like He knows about everything you do, specially the bad things?

OLD MAN   Ah, that's a big problem.

MARY   What?

OLD MAN   God's recognition of evil. You see, if God wishes to overcome evil and He can't, then He's impotent. If He wants to overcome evil and He doesn't, then *He* is evil himself. And if He has the power and the will to overcome evil, how is it He allows us to be exposed and infected by it?

MARY   (*Totally confused*)   Hey, what'a you give me all that stuff? I just asked a simple question.

OLD MAN   The answer to your question is I don't know.

MARY   All *right*. Why didn't you say so? It takes three words, and you gotta go through all that jazz.

OLD MAN   It *is* much better to say it that way, isn't it? (*Silence*)

21

MARY Most old people I ask about things like that, they know it all. Oh boy, they know everything about everything.

OLD MAN One of the misfortunes of age.

MARY (*Watches him write*) Hey, what's that jazz you're writing all the time?

OLD MAN Oh, it's just a journal of my impressions of the day.

MARY You some kind of writer, then?

OLD MAN I'm not a teacher, and I'm not a writer.

MARY Then what are you?

OLD MAN Nothing.

MARY How could you be nothing? I mean, everybody's something: farmers, and truck drivers, and doctors. How could you be nothing? Unless you're a bum.

OLD MAN I'll settle for that.

MARY Yeah, well that's what I figured the first place. (*The* OLD MAN *continues to write*) Hey, what do you put down?

OLD MAN All kinds of things: the colors of sunsets, the smell of breezes, the feel of wine sting in my mouth, and the taste of wild beach plums, the way the jasmine comes down out of the canyons on damp nights to drown you in sweetness, the fog catching in the trees, like a woman's hair . . .

MARY What for?

OLD MAN Well, the days are very precious to me now. They're so full of strangeness and wonder . . . so brief. I don't want them to escape me. I want to fix, remember everything. (*He chuckles*) It's like grabbing the day by the scruff of the neck and saying, "You're not getting away that easy." Things move so quickly, now. At night, by the fire, I open my book and read. It slows things up a little. I know it's kind of silly. I've even put you down in here.

MARY Yeah? Hey, no kidding?

OLD MAN That's right.

MARY What'd you say about me?

OLD MAN You wouldn't be interested.

MARY Yes I would.

OLD MAN I don't think I'd better . . .

MARY Sure, sure, I know. You said I was a raunch.

23

OLD MAN   No. It's just that the entries are very personal.

MARY   Ok, skip it! (*She walks to stage left and looks out at the ocean*) What time is it?

OLD MAN   Four forty-five.

MARY   Thanks a bunch.
(*The* OLD MAN *looks at her for a long moment. He takes a drink of wine, opens his journal, and reads*)

OLD MAN   I have just learned her name is Mary. She is about fifteen.

MARY   Sixteen.

OLD MAN (*Makes the correction*)   Sixteen. And very, very lovely. (MARY *turns toward him, surprised*) There is a quality about her that reminds me of Lisa. Perhaps it is her eyes, or the line of her cheek, or her embarrassment every time she laughs . . . as if she had to make apology for these. Perhaps it is a combination of these things. She carries a certain sadness that is quite undefinable. It gives her a dimension beyond her years. She is at the same time old and young; wise and idiot. Yes, that's it. She is Huxley's lay idiot of nature, attuning herself to the days ahead. It is painful for me to see her. She evokes such memories. It is painful.
(*He closes the book and looks up*)

MARY   Gee . . .

OLD MAN   I told you it was personal.

Amy Taubin and Franchot Tone as MARY and the OLD MAN

MARY   Hey, did you really mean what you put down there about me being pretty?

OLD MAN   Yes.

MARY   Boy, that makes me feel funny.

OLD MAN   Why?

MARY   Well, nobody ever called me . . . well what you called me there.

OLD MAN   Lovely?

MARY   Yeah?

OLD MAN   It's true.

MARY   Aw, come on . . .

OLD MAN (*Crossing his heart*) Cross my heart and . . . cross my heart.

MARY   God, it makes me feel funny. I don't know what to say.

OLD MAN   Don't say anything.

MARY   Who's Lisa?

OLD MAN   A girl, a beautiful enigma I once loved in my youth and still do in my sunsets. That's pretty good.

(*He opens his book and writes*) In my senile sunsets. Good alliteration.

MARY   Hey, I bet you were a real lover.

OLD MAN   Oh, no . . . (*Embarrassed*)

MARY   Aw, sure. Come on. I bet you were a big make-out.

OLD MAN   Why do you say that?

MARY   You got the look.

OLD MAN   What look?

MARY   Just the look. I can tell. Admit it. You were a big make-out.

OLD MAN   Oh, no . . .

MARY   Hey, come on. I mean, what the hell, I give it to you straight about the initiation, right?

OLD MAN   Right.

MARY   So?

OLD MAN   (*Grinning with embarrassment*) Well . . . I . . . I . . . didn't do so bad.

MARY   (*Laughing*) Yeah, you see? I told you. I knew it. Come on, didn't I tell you? Yeah, try to pull a fast one.

I can tell. (*The* OLD MAN *joins her laughter*) Yeah, think you're pretty tricky.

OLD MAN (*Still laughing*)　Well I didn't mean to . . .

MARY　Yeah, I got your number. (*They both laugh*) Hey, read that last part about me, again. You know, about nature and stuff.

OLD MAN (*Reading*)　She is at the same time old and young; wise and idiot . . .

MARY　I'm not an idiot.

OLD MAN　The way I use the word is not in its normal meaning.

MARY　An idiot's an idiot.

OLD MAN　No. Here it means a person on the brink of life, just at the threshold of emotions.

MARY　Boy, you sure say things funny. What else you got in there?

OLD MAN　Lots of things.

MARY　Read me more.

OLD MAN　I don't know. I've never read any of this to anyone before.

MARY　No kidding? You mean I'm the first?

OLD MAN   The very first.

MARY   Then you *gotta!* Come on. What else you got to do?

OLD MAN (*Looking at her closely*)   Nothing. Nothing at all. (*He turns to the front of the journal and begins reading*) Ten o'clock, Monday. I am looking at one of these coastal sierras. It is very distant and very high. And I am struck with awe at the thought of the great pyramid of Gizeh; a man-made pile of two million blocks of stone, each weighing two and a half tons. I can't think what prompted this thought, except on getting out of bed this morning I felt the twinge of an old rupture.

MARY (*Breaks into laughter. She slaps her hand to her mouth, trying to stifle it*)   Oh . . . oh that's too much. Is that wild!
        (*The* OLD MAN *is bewildered by her laughter at first, then joins it*)

OLD MAN   I never thought of it as being funny.

MARY   That is really wild. Go ahead.

OLD MAN (*Reading*)   Twelve o'clock, Tuesday. I have found some stones this morning whose whiteness reminds me of the tomb of Vittorio Emmanuel in Rome, and all of its space-consuming ugliness. It doubles as a monument to thousands of names and obscenities scribbled on the columns and walls of the upper loggias. Poor Vittorio. Glory can never escape a little of the plebeian's phlegm. Ahem . . . this next entry is not exactly what you might call proper.

MARY   Come on. Come off that. What'a you think, I'm a square or something?

OLD MAN (*Clears his throat*)   I remember inspecting the gigantic statue of Emmanuel. The horse upon which he rides has testicles the size of watermelons. The Italians have always known how to avoid subtleties when symbolizing the virility of the race.
(*He clears his throat nervously*)

MARY (*Snickering*)   Wow, is that a dirty one. You're too much.

OLD MAN (*Reads the next entry silently, then looks up*) I think that's enough.

MARY   Aw, come on.

OLD MAN   No . . . I think I've read . . .

MARY   Just one more. Come on. I won't ask you for any more after this.

OLD MAN (*Smiling*)   All right.
(*He begins leafing through the pages*)

MARY   Oh no. Don't pick it out. I know. You won't read the good stuff. You gotta do it this way. Close the book. (*He shrugs and closes it*) Now close your eyes.

OLD MAN Why?

MARY (*Giggling*) Come on now, close them. (*He does so*) Now open the book and read right where you are and no changing to another place. Ok?

OLD MAN Ok. (*He opens the book and begins reading*) Friday, ten A.M. . . . I have just come from the beach. The anemones are exploding on the hillsides among the silky wet green of ice plants. They remind me of . . . of . . .
      (*He reads on silently, his face becoming grave*)

MARY Go ahead.

OLD MAN (*Turning pages*) This one isn't very interesting. I'll read something else.

MARY No! See, that's what I mean? I knew you'd do that. You gotta read the one you opened to.

OLD MAN Why?

MARY Because.

OLD MAN Why?

MARY Oh, cripes, because you *said* you would.

OLD MAN (*Absently, to himself*) That's important, isn't it: doing what we say we will do?

MARY Sure.

OLD MAN (*Finds his original place and reads*) . . . silky wet green of the ice plants. They remind me of . . . of those on the beach at Naxos. I am remembering a morning in August. Lisa and I are lying in the sand. The heat is suffocating, complete . . . unrelenting. It invades my body so deeply, I'm chilled by it. The sun . . . sun is an arc light penetrating my lids so that the shapes I see on the underside of them are ringed with prismatic rainbows. She lies near me, silent. The surf whispers and grates through the small stones in the sand. It is done. She is going away tomorrow morning, somewhere into the world. Somewhere into time and void and the no-faces of cities. And we lie quietly in the Naxos sun. Cold with the sun . . . cold. God how she obsesses me. We will couple tonight. And in it there will be an urgency to compress the caresses of the two years we have known each other. The urgency and the futility. Strange how the colors of anemones should evoke such thoughts. (*Still reading*) God . . . oh, God. It has been ten years . . . since . . . I have felt the touch of a woman. Since . . . I caressed since . . . since . . . (*There are tears in his eyes. He closes the book*) I'm sorry. I . . .

MARY Gee . . . Gosh, that's ok. I didn't know it would shake you up like that.

OLD MAN Neither did I.

MARY You ever see that chick again?

OLD MAN No.

MARY And you been alone since then?

OLD MAN (*A bitter laugh*) Oh, no. That was many years ago. I was still young and the world was wide and wonderful.

MARY And lots of other chicks around?

OLD MAN Lots.

MARY How's come you never got married and had kids and all that?

OLD MAN Oh, I wanted to but I had a ghost holding me back, hovering over my shoulder, wherever I went. I lived and loved. When I say *love*, I mean in the physical sense. You understand?

MARY Uh huh.

OLD MAN I searched out the faces and voices of the world, looking, waiting, thinking, "This year it's going to happen. I will turn the corner in New York or Algeciras, or Rabát, and she will be there; the one, the real one. Through the streets of decaying cities, looking . . . looking. You don't know what that kind of hunger is. I never found the face, the voice.

MARY Why?

OLD MAN My ghost had been with me too long. I'd been looking for an idea, not a person; somewhere out there, external, I thought it would find me . . . Stupid! How classically stupid to think it would happen *to* me . . . I had . . . well . . . I had been looking for love too long with none inside. I never found it. And that's why I'm here, alone, looking at sunsets and scribbling the hiero-glyphics of some confused, demented cretin.

MARY   Boy, that's too much.

OLD MAN   I suppose it is. We can't get what we don't possess. Oh, we can play the games but they seem to kill the seed of what we might have really had to give.

MARY   You mean if you play a game with what you really feel inside, then it'll always be just a game and nothing else?

OLD MAN   You say it better.

MARY   Uh huh. Yeah.
(*There is a long silence. They are both within their own thoughts.* MARY *looks at the* OLD MAN)

OLD MAN (*His face tightens with some painful memory, and he speaks absently*) There are certain moments, on arising early morning, looking out the window at the gray sleeping world, when suddenly your arm touches the gauze curtain and every nerve in your body spasms with the memory of skin, faces, lips, the feel of your body on another, the look of the whiteness of sheets in the half-light of dawn. And suddenly you want to love. And the loneliness drives so deep, inside you, it has no ending. And you feel yourself sinking . . . sinking inside, back to those lost hours of color and music and laughter, and the sweet salt smell of those brief obliterations. (*He*

33

looks up to find her staring at him) I'm sorry. I guess I ramble a lot.
(*Silence*)

MARY   Then there's nothing for you. I mean nothing but being alone. Gee . . .

OLD MAN   There are compensations. Nature has its own special language. Once you learn it, there's some communication.

MARY   You ought to do something.

OLD MAN   What?

MARY   Don't you have a TV or a radio?

OLD MAN   No.

MARY   Well, you ought to get one. Do *something*. Move someplace where you could meet people.

OLD MAN   I've met them all.

MARY   Even a radio'd be something. I mean, like you could listen to the news and music and like that.

OLD MAN   I'm not interested in the news.

MARY   How about music? Wait a minute. Listen to this.
(*She turns her radio on to some rock-'n'-roll music*)

OLD MAN (*Listens a moment*)   Is that music?

34

MARY   Are you kidding? This is the greatest.
(*She begins to twist. The* OLD MAN *watches, confused and amused by her antics*)

OLD MAN   That's very interesting.

MARY (*As she dances*)   It's the twist. Grind, grind, grind.

OLD MAN   The twist?

MARY   I forgot, you been in orbit. (*She demonstrates*)
My gym teacher says it's very healthy.

OLD MAN   It looks dangerous.

MARY (*Laughs*)   Here, come here. I'll show you how.

OLD MAN   Are you serious?

MARY   Sure. Come on.

OLD MAN   Oh, no . . .

MARY (*She takes him by the hands, and leads him down
right*)   Come on. Don't be such an old grouch. It's easy.

OLD MAN   No, I couldn't . . .

MARY   Aw, you wanna be a drag all your life? Look. You
just stand in one spot, like this, with your feet apart,
and your right leg a little ahead of your left. (*She demonstrates*) Come on.

35

OLD MAN (*Grins, and assumes the stance reluctantly*) Like this?

MARY Ok. Now make a fist with both hands. (*He clenches his fists*) Now just kinda make out like you're punching from the hips. Like this.
(*She demonstrates*)

OLD MAN This all right?
(*He extends his arms and punches*)

MARY No. Bend your arms. Just from the elbows. (*The OLD MAN makes the adjustment*) That's it! You got it! Now while you keep doing that, just start twisting your body. Watch. (*She demonstrates*) Try it. (*The OLD MAN begins awkwardly, and forgets to move his arms*) No! Keep punching. (*He moves his arms*) Crazy.

OLD MAN I'm embarrassed.

MARY You're doing great. (*She dances along with him*) That's it. Crazy. Back an' forth. Yeah. Now twist more. Grind it up down there.

OLD MAN Are we dancing or making coffee?

MARY (*Laughs*) Oh, you're too much. Yeah, that's it. (*She turns the music up*) You got it. Watch me. Watch. (*He tries to imitate her*) Isn't this a gas? You ever do anything like this?

OLD MAN Never. (*He laughs with a joy that speaks of a release of all his loneliness. MARY joins him in laughter.*

The music blares) I wonder what anyone would say if
they saw us?

MARY   Who cares? I mean, do you care?

OLD MAN   Not a bit. Grind, grind, grind.
(*They both laugh. Suddenly, the* OLD MAN *winces
with pain. He stops dancing. His hand goes to his
chest. He gasps for breath*)

MARY   Hey, what's the matter?

OLD MAN   Nothing . . . nothing . . .

MARY   You sick or something?

OLD MAN   If . . . if I could just sit down.

MARY   Sure. (*He sits, and takes a bottle of small, white
pills from his pocket, opens it, and places one of the
pills under his tongue.* MARY, *silent and shaken, watches
him. A long moment passes. His breathing becomes
easier. He smiles weakly at her*) Ok?

OLD MAN   Ok.

MARY   Wow, don't scare me like that.

OLD MAN   I'm sorry. It's this stupid heart. Ridiculous.
Ridiculous, the things it does.

MARY   Why didn't you tell me you were sick?

OLD MAN   It's not important. I'm all right now.

MARY   Yeah, but you shouldn't be dancing and stuff like that.
   (*She turns off the radio*)

OLD MAN   I'm all right, I told you. And . . . and I'm glad we twisted. Very glad. (*A pause*) Did I do pretty well?

MARY   You were fabulous, but you scared the hell out of me.

OLD MAN   I'm sorry.

MARY   That's what my grandpa had: a bad heart, I mean. Boy, he couldn't do nothing. He just walked around the house like a zombie. He didn't say much. He was always kinda grouchy anyway. But his eyes seemed to get real big. And he just kept looking at everything. Just looking and looking . . .

OLD MAN   (*Tensing*)   Let's forget it, shall we?

MARY   Geeze, I'll never forget that. One morning we're in the kitchen eating and he falls over, his head right in the Wheaties. God, it was terrible. Then they bring in an oxygen tent and all kinds of bottles with stuff in them: blood and white stuff, with tubes and needles stuck in his arms and feet and neck. God, it was creepy. I used to look at him under the tent, just laying there, not knowing what was happening to him. And his big eyes just looking and looking all the time.

38

OLD MAN (*Trying to hide his panic*) Let's forget it. I'm sure it was very bad. Do you mind . . . ?

MARY I was in the room when it happened. His eyes got all shiny, and then he makes a funny sound, like he's gargling or something, and just lays there dead, with his eyes open . . . looking . . . and looking . . . and . . .

OLD MAN (*Unable to take it any longer*) I don't want to hear! I don't want to *know* about your grandfather!

MARY Oh, gee, sure. Hey, I'm sorry. I guess old people don't like to hear about things like that.

OLD MAN (*Sharply*) There are other things to talk about!

MARY Ok. You don't have to get mad. I'll shut up.

OLD MAN That's fine!

MARY You're too much. Is it my fault you're sick? What'a you yelling at me for?

OLD MAN I didn't yell at you.

MARY Sure you did. Just like my grandpa. You try to be nice and right away he'd get grouchy. Boy, you old people are all the same.

OLD MAN (*Vehemently*) What do you know? What do you *know* about it? You think I'm different from you? You think I don't see the sky as you do, don't think or need or desire? *Old?* What's *old?* Am I different because

39

my skin hangs loose and I have less teeth? Did you ever stop to think what's here, (*He touches his face*) behind the face, behind the skin and bone? *Did* you? I'm *alive* in here! Can't you see that, you stupid little girl? I'm still *me,* trapped in this cage of time. Me, loving on the beaches of Naxos, seeing anemones, drinking, fighting, hating, crashing through the world with my hands in its guts! Don't talk to me about *death.* I'm alive. I have nothing in common with *this* (*He pulls at the skin of his arm*), or *this!* (*He pulls at the skin of his face*) Nothing! *Nothing!* (*He turns away from her.* MARY *stands, looking at him, shocked. The* OLD MAN *is unnerved, shaking. A long moment passes. The* OLD MAN *takes the five-dollar bill and holds it out to her, without looking at her*) Here, take your five dollars and get out of here. (MARY *is silent*) Well, take it!

MARY   What time is it?

OLD MAN (*Looking at his watch*)   Five-thirty. What's the difference?

MARY   I can't. There's five more minutes on our bet.

OLD MAN   It doesn't matter.

MARY   It does to me. What'a you think I'm some kind of crook or something?
(*The* OLD MAN *puts the bill back into the book. There is a long awkward silence. He cannot look at her.* MARY *continues staring at him. Finally, he turns and looks at her*)

OLD MAN Why are you staring at me?

MARY Gee . . . what you said. I never really thought
about it like that before. I mean like . . . well like being
the same inside. I just never thought about it. I'm sorry
I made you mad at me. I'm sorry about talking about . . .
Oh, God, I'm dumb. I'm really dumb.

OLD MAN (*Regaining some of his composure. He forces a
smile*) It's . . . well . . . it's all right.

MARY You sure?

OLD MAN Yes.

MARY You're not mad at me?

OLD MAN I'm not mad.
        (*Silence*)

MARY Anyway, you learned how to twist.
        (*They both laugh*)

OLD MAN (*Looking out to sea*) Look, there's a stratum
of rose that's come into the sky, now. How very beautiful. (*He jots in his book.* MARY *looks at him for a
long moment, then walks directly in front of him, block-
ing his view. She seems to have made up her mind about
something. The* OLD MAN *looks up her, surprised by her
expression*) What's the matter?

MARY I . . . I wanna kiss you.

OLD MAN What?

MARY   Gee, I don't know. It's funny. I just feel like I wanna kiss you. Would you let me?

OLD MAN   I . . . I don't. Oh, Mary, a peck on the cheek heals no . . .

MARY   I don't mean like that. I mean really. Don't you want me to?

OLD MAN (*Turning away from her*)   I . . . I can't . . .

MARY   Let me, please. I want to. (*They look at each other for a long moment. The* OLD MAN *nods.* MARY *walks to him and kneels down in front of him. She moves her face close to him. He turns his face away so she can kiss him on the cheek*) No. On the lips. (*He turns and looks at her.* MARY *kisses him on the lips. The kiss is long. The* OLD MAN's *hand comes up and caresses her hair gently.* MARY *moves back away from him, looking at him*) Hey, whatsa matter?

OLD MAN   Forgive me. I . . . I . . .
    (CHUCK *enters suddenly, through the thicket, and sees them. He runs to them*)

CHUCK (*Pulling* MARY *away from the* OLD MAN)   Christ! What're you *doing*?

MARY   Chuck, I . . .

CHUCK   You, you, dirty old bastard. How could you touch her? How *could* you?

MARY (*Trying to scream through his violence*) Chuck, it was me . . . *me!* I wanted him to!

OLD MAN Now look here, boy . . .

CHUCK (*Punching the* OLD MAN *about the face, each blow punctuating his words*) Shut up, you ugly old shit! You've had it, Pops. Oh boy, have you had it. How could you *touch* her?

MARY It was *me!* (*She tries to pull* CHUCK *away from the* OLD MAN *who can do nothing but feebly try to protect his face with his arms*) He's sick! Don't! Chuck!

CHUCK (*Punching*) I knew you were following us. You were after her! I knew it.

MARY Stop it. Oh, God . . . stop it. You'll kill him!

CHUCK Son-of-a-bitch. Old ugly son-of-a-*bitch!*
(*He stands away, breathing hard. The* OLD MAN *is on the ground, bleeding from the nose and mouth.* MARY *stands looking at him, sobbing*)

MARY Jesus . . . oh Jesus God!

CHUCK (*Turning to her*) You *let* him. You . . . you . . .
(*He turns and runs off into the thicket*)

MARY Chuck!
(*She runs after him to the edge of the thicket, then turns to see the* OLD MAN *lifting himself painfully*)

43

OLD MAN (*Smiling weakly*) He . . . he's very strong.

MARY (*Looking at his battered face*) Oh Jesus God.

OLD MAN You'd better catch him before he leaves.

MARY But . . .

OLD MAN I'll survive. (*He takes out the five-dollar bill*) Here.

MARY Aw, no . . .

OLD MAN A bet's a bet.
(*She crosses to him, crying, and takes the bill*)

MARY Thanks.

OLD MAN I didn't really expect him to come back, you know?

MARY Aw, hell, I knew that. (*The* OLD MAN *nods*) I'm . . . I'm glad you were here.

OLD MAN Thank you.

MARY (*She picks up the blanket and moves to the edge of the thicket. She turns*) So long, mister.

OLD MAN Mary? (*She turns back to him*) Did I really twist good?

MARY Fabulous. You're . . . you're something else. Really something else.

(*She stands for a long moment, shaking her head, crying silently*)

OLD MAN (*Smiling at her*) You'll miss your ride. (*She turns and runs off. The* OLD MAN *looks at the spot where she stood for a long moment. He shakes his head. He opens his journal, wets the end of his pencil and writes*) A remarkable thing happened to me today. A visitation from a god. I . . . I don't think I shall quite recover from it. No! That's enough about that. (*He takes a last sip from his bottle. He turns it up. It is empty*) Twinkle, twinkle, little grape. . . . (*He drops the bottle. He looks at his watch*) Five forty-five. The light changes so quickly. The faded rose has become almost scarlet. Above it, the mauve and vermilions have turned crepuscular . . . as the twilight compresses them into the sea. Twilight. . . . (*He puts his face in his hands, sobbing*) Fool! Fool! Did you have to bring it all back again? Did you have to feel it all *again*? There isn't enough pain in the memories? Fool! Fool! (*He pulls the skin of his face and arms*) What right do you have to her dimension of time? Fool! Dirty old man. (*Over and over, he hits himself on the face and mouth*) What *right*? Fool! Dirty . . . dirty . . . dirty . . . old . . . old! (*He stops. He looks up at the sky. He is crying softly. He asks the question of the silence and void*) What right? (*Then, as the curtain closes*) Eh . . . eh . . . eh . . . eh?

Curtain

Sarah and The Sax

To Peggy, for her kindness, her beauty, and her belief.

Scene: A park bench, the morning of a summer day, the present. There is a tree behind the bench and shrubbery to the left of it. A waste can is downstage right.

At Rise: SARAH *is seated, crocheting a doily. She is a plump Jewish woman of about fifty-five. There is a shopping bag to one side of her feet. Birds chirp, unseen, high in the secret green of trees.* SARAH *looks up, savoring the sound. She smiles. An ambulance siren wails by. Her look changes to one of concern and worry. The sound of the siren fades.* SARAH *goes back to her crocheting. Her attention then turns toward the sound of someone mumbling, offstage right. The mumbling becomes louder until finally* THE SAX *enters. He is a Negro, about thirty, with a few scraggly hairs of chin beard. He wears sunglasses and is barefoot. His tattered old sweatshirt and denims are encrusted with grime of almost geologic age, and he carries an old saxophone on a string, fastened around his neck. He also carries a ragged tote bag.*

THE SAX (*Mumbling to himself as he crosses to the bench*) Tom Mix, pick up sticks, get my licks, sweat my fix, watch the dicks—Tracy. Con the hicks. (*He sits. He is completely oblivious to* SARAH *who watches him with unmasked curiosity.* THE SAX *is in his Elysium. He is away, gone, floating in a world of his own making*) How's tricks, Dorothy Dix?

SARAH (*Thinking he is talking to her*) The name is Sarah Nodelman and if I should tell you the truth, I'm not so

51

good. I got a leg (*She taps her knee*) it hurts so much with the humidity, it's talking to me since nine o'clock.

THE SAX (*Looks at her with surprise, then turns away, blotting her from his consciousness. He speaks to himself*) Crash, into the circle of golden silence comes this yapper makin' like the aspirin commercials on telaversion. Man, they're droppin' off the telephone wires! (*He takes out an immaculately clean rag and carefully unfolds it. He begins to polish his saxophone*)

SARAH (*Putting down the doily*) I'm not looking at the television for two days, now. Something is wrong with the tube. Everybody's got only a half a head. Two days now I'm waiting for the man to come fix. You know what's the trouble? Nobody is caring. They all make too much money. You think the man who fixes is worrying because I got to sit lookin' at everybody with a half a head? Believe me, he don't. Oh, but last week it was beautiful. I was looking until sometimes one o'clock. I saw . . .

THE SAX Saw! *Saw!* Hack saw, band saw, back saw, bone saw, hand saw, jig saw, crosscut, rip saw, wood saw, buzz saw, see *saw!* Et tu, Brute? (*He punctuates with one short honk on his saxophone. Silence.* SARAH *smiles*)

SARAH That's a very nice poem. I heard that one before.

THE SAX (*To her, without looking at her*) Dig, baby, am I telepathizin' with you? I mean, you a yapper and you makin' with sounds that are hangin' up my tympanic membrane. Cool it. You know what I mean? 'Cause the jazz you comin' off with is buggin' me. I'm tellin' you, I am *bugged!*

SARAH (*Looking up into the tree*) Yeah, a couple fell on me. They're eating the leaves. It's a shame. Maybe you should move this way a little so you won't be disturbed. (THE SAX *moves to the opposite side of the bench, away from her*) Yeah, that's a very nice poem. *Et tu,* you brute. That's from Jakespeare. I know. Sometimes they're playing also him on the television. One time even with Marlon Branden.

THE SAX (*To some unseen listener*) Ooo, daddy, this ananda killer is too much. (*To* SARAH) Wee oo, baby you a rectangle. Get yourself a Guru. (*He finishes wiping his saxophone, then plays a short passage, pointing the saxophone up into the tree behind the bench. The music is clean, highly complex, virtuosic*) Hey, you little chickadees, you dig that? My answer to Buxtehude! (*A short honk*) Yeah, an' that's for Honegger, Hindemith, Schoenberg, shoo-fly, and all them finger-poppin' daddies!

SARAH It's nice you can play music. You should be thankful for such a talent.

THE SAX (*Turned away from her, his hand cupped to his ear*) Where *is* that sound comin' from?

SARAH My son Herbie, when he was in high school, he used to play the ocarina.

THE SAX   I don't care if the cat blew piccolo.

SARAH   A piccolo, that's right! Only smaller. Oh, it was nice. He used to play for me "Home on the Range." An' you wanna know something? He never learned music. All with the numbers. All day long, up and down the house. (*To the tune of "Home on the Range"*) Three three, four, five, six. Four, three, five, six, seven . . . A very gifted boy. All with the numbers, I'm telling you.

THE SAX   Drag . . . drag. Who gonna give you a gig with a ocarina?

SARAH   Can you play "Home on the Range" on that saxingphone?

THE SAX   Wee ooo, it's a break from Bellevue, and this one's the *leader!* Head for the BMT!
(*He blows one short honk on his saxophone*)

SARAH   Maybe you don't like that kind of music. You look like one of those jazzy musicians. Are you one of those bee-boppers?

THE SAX   Yeah, well, you know, baby. You gotta blow. You wail, swing, hurry on back, screech through a few Cs till ya got pimples on your back.

SARAH   My Herbie had pimples on his face till he was eighteen. It made him so bashful, he wouldn't go to none of the dances. But they went away as soon as he went in with the army. Just like medicine.

THE SAX Drag . . . drag, mamala. Army's a drag. They don't got no pizza.

SARAH What a happy letter I got from him when they went away. He was like a new person.

THE SAX Yeah, man. How you gonna swing without pizza? What a wig. Suck all that mozzarella down your gut. Yeah, baby. Pizza! Greasy, easy, slidy, sloppy, sticky, pizza! Gimme, gimme, man. I dunk it in my Bosco! (*A high-school cheer*) Yea, pizza! (*A short honk on his saxophone. Silence*) Viva Zapata, and pizza!

SARAH You like pizza?

THE SAX (*Shouting to his unseen listener*) Never mind the BMT! Head for the Empire State! It's our only chance!

SARAH With Herbie, knish. I make them very light. Some people, let me tell you, like rubber they come out. You know something, it's funny by the store I see now they got frozen knish. What a world.

THE SAX (*Shouting*) Pizza! Pizza! I like it! Greasy, cheesy, slimy, suck the mozzarella off, pizza! I want it! I love it! Gimme, gimme! It's cool! (*He plays a passage projecting pizza. It is music that slides. It is woven with old Italian themes*) Yeah!

SARAH (*Impressed with the music*) That's very nice. But you shouldn't eat it cool. It makes a heavy ball in your stomach and what happens? You should pardon the expression, constipation.

THE SAX (*Picks up an imaginary telephone and dials. Then, secretly into the phone*) Hello, FBI? This is the blob. I wanna report an enemy agent. (SARAH *looks around*) That's right. She carryin' a bomb. A mouth bomb. It keeps goin' off and I can't stop it. The populus is dyin' in the streets. (SARAH *is confused by his antics*) Ok. Check. (*He hangs up, then turns to* SARAH *and says with gravity*) Ok, baby, your cop-out days are over. They're sendin' down their best man with an electric chair. (*He sticks his tongue out at her, then plays a fanfare. Then, in a March of Time voice*) And so Jack Legstrong brings still another enemy to justice in his never-ending fight for God and country! The blob strikes again!
(*A short honk*)

SARAH (*Shaking her head*) I give him good advice and he calls the FBI on me!

THE SAX Advice! Advice. Add the vise. The vice of adding the vise, twice vice. Unwise to squeeze the vise. A bad vice of lice and mice playing dice with people, like the cloud daddy with no face. (*Sharply, to* SARAH) Who asked you? I mean, who really *asked* you, baby?

SARAH (*Hurt*) So what is it against the law to give a little suggestion how you should eat?

THE SAX (*Mumbling into the opening of his saxophone*) Hey, man, you dig what this chick is puttin' down?

Clarence Williams III and Ruth White as THE SAX and SARAH

They the dangerous ones. You hep? On guard, dig? Or like the French say, *E pluribus unum.*

SARAH   Listen, from the way you look, a few suggestions you could stand.

THE SAX (*To his saxophone*)   Make out she's not here.

SARAH   For example what's the matter you can't afford a pair of shoes? You know you could get a jawlock walking like that besides it being unsanitary? And what is it a new style with the dirty clothes? Fifteen cents in the launderette and you could look like a human person.

THE SAX (*Closing his eyes*)   She ain't here. She ain't here.

SARAH   The beard, that's all right. I know all the jazzy musicians have them.

THE SAX (*Sarcastically*)   Thank you.

SARAH   You're welcome, I'm sure. Believe me, you would do yourself a favor if you looked a little better. You should see my Herbie, now. Socks and shirt changed every day. Spotless. Even on the weekend, when he don't work. His wife and children, the same thing. Clean like a pin. Neat. Nice. You know he got his last promotion because of that? What should your mother say if she saw you looking like this; like a bum? A nice talented boy.

THE SAX (*Looks at her. Then into his saxophone*)   Hey, man, I gotta talk to you. (*He talks into the opening,*

*secretively. We cannot hear his words, only a mumble.
He waits a moment, then sticks the mouthpiece into his
ear and listens. He nods affirmation)* Uh huh. I'm hep.
(He smiles) Wail, man *(His face goes serious. He
speaks into the opening once more, this time with a
British accent)* Squadron leader Wembly to command.
*(He gets up and moves away from Sarah, then turns,
pointing the saxophone at her)* Approaching target.
Target in sight! *(The mouthpiece goes to his ear. He
nods)* Roger and out. *(He approaches* SARAH *and anni-
hilates her with short, machine gun blasts on the saxophone.* SARAH *stares at him, shaking her head at this
strange behavior.* THE SAX *finishes his attack and sits on
the bench once more. He speaks into the opening of the
saxophone)* Mission accomplished. *(He lets* SARAH *have
one last shot, then shakes hands with the mouthpiece)*
Good show, old man. Well done.

SARAH   What's that supposed to mean?

THE SAX *(Shouting)*   Quiet! Silence! You can't speak!
You're dead!

SARAH   So I'll be a talking ghost if you don't mind. You
should be ashamed. Listen, there's enough people in the
world being killed without you should make a joke. At
your age such games are not so funny.

THE SAX *(A preacher's voice)*   And I say to you, brethren,
judgment is at hand. Retribution lies in your liverwurst.
Dig? "For that which is born, death is certain, and for
the dead birth is certain. Therefore grieve not over that

which is unavoidable." Chapter two, verse twenty-seven, Upanishads.

SARAH What's that?

THE SAX Zen.

SARAH Ten?

THE SAX Zen! Zen!

SARAH Oh, Sen-Sen. I never use it. A little parsley, it's enough.

THE SAX (*Screaming*) Bwana! Bwana! Boys, they *go!* All 'fraid! Me 'fraid! (*He points to* SARAH, *speaking excitedly to some unseen companion*) White witch doctor. Bad juju. No! No, me go! Me 'fraid! She make bad devils. Even kill simba. Me go! Me *'fraid* (*His tone changes. His is* THE SAX *once more*) 'Course, man, if you was to lay a double sawbuck on me, I'd stick around. Yeah, baby, an' for an extra five, I'd get them cats back to carry all this jazz. Oh no! No Diner's card! The cash. (*He pantomimes taking the money*) Ok. Great, man. Oh, one more thing. From now on you carry your own rifle, dig? (*He jumps up and down and hollers some made-up African gibberish to an unseen group*) I don't know what it means, either, but it sounds good.
(*A short honk on the saxophone. He sits.* SARAH, *who has been watching all this, shakes her head*)

SARAH Listen, making fun of me, I don't mind. But if the police see you doing such crazy things, they'll take you away for sure, believe me. In five minutes you're in the FBI, you're in the Air Force, and then all of a sudden you're Jungle Jim. What kind of a thing is that for your age?

THE SAX   Age, smage. There is no age. Dig, baby. I am the embryo of the universe. I am the fetus shrinking into prenatal reality. I am the amoeba, and before that, water. And before that, the idea. I am ananda. I am aksa! (*Angrily*) So will you quit *buggin'* me? I don't want to talk to you, dig? Keep your helpful hints to yourself. You hip? Just take your straitjackets and blast off! Quit *buggin'* me!

> (SARAH *is hurt, but she does not move.* THE SAX *continues to clean his saxophone, ignoring her. He moves his bare feet back and forth, on their heels, as he works.* SARAH *looks at his feet, then at him, then back at his feet. She reaches for her purse and extracts three one-dollar bills. She straightens them out and holds them out to* THE SAX)

SARAH   It's not much, but at least a pair of sneakers you'll be able to buy. (THE SAX *looks at the money, then at* SARAH, *then turns away.* SARAH *shrugs and puts the money into the opening of the saxophone*) So don't be ashamed somebody should want to help you a little. (THE SAX *turns and sees the bills. He extracts them, gets up, takes a few steps forward, and places them on the ground. He walks back to the bench in silence, sits, and turns away from her. He wipes the inside of his saxophone as if it had been contaminated.* SARAH *looks at* THE SAX, *then at the money on the ground. There is a long silence. Finally, she gets up, goes to the money, picks it up, returns to the bench and sits. She puts the money back into her purse. A long moment passes. She looks at* THE SAX) I'm sorry. I didn't mean to offend you. (THE SAX *remains turned away. She shakes her head*) What a world. You think you know how to do things, you don't. Everything is changing. Just now I don't know if I offered you the three dollars for your good or for mine. You got a right to be insulted.

(*She shakes her head*)

THE SAX (*Quietly, still turned away from her*) Can it, baby. Father Confessor is out to lunch.

(SARAH *smiles, then goes back to her crocheting. Another siren wails by. She shakes her head, sadly*)

SARAH What a life. Every minute, somebody's got a trag-edy. (*The chirping of the birds fades in as the sound of the siren diminishes.* SARAH *smiles again*) This is such a nice park. Little? Yes. But so nice. Especially in the morning, like now. Eleven years I'm coming here on Thursday after my shopping before going home. I don't live here. Uptown, Ninety-second Street and West End. You know where that is? (THE SAX *does not respond*) They got a park up there, too. Along Riverside Drive. But what kind of a place is it? You walk across the street and you're in the Catskills. It's the country. Who wants to be in the Catskills and in New York at the same time? For me, one thing or the other. Here it's nice. You got all the buildings and not so much grass like a forest. You know you're still in the city. I do my shopping on Houston Street. Such a wonderful butcher he's there.

61

Listen, if it seems like a long way to come, I'll tell you something. I wouldn't spend a nickel on those crooks, uptown. You know something? Listen, I'll tell you something save you a lot of grief. Every butcher between Twenty-ninth Street and One Hundred and Second is high.

(THE SAX *turns and stares at her*)

THE SAX (*His eyes wide with shock*) Hey, baby, you puttin' me on?

SARAH I'm not putting you on or off. It's the truth.

THE SAX (*A spirit of conspiracy*) Are you sure?

SARAH Certainly I'm sure. It's like a club. One week I went to a whole bunch of them. And you know what? High! Every one of them. But not just a little.

THE SAX (*Incredulous*) *All* of them?

SARAH All!

THE SAX Man, there must be a shipment come in on a cattle boat.

SARAH I don't know how they can do it.

THE SAX Well, they can afford it. They must be makin' a lot of bread.

SARAH What's the matter you don't listen? I said *butchers*, not bakers.

THE SAX Yeah, yeah!

SARAH Oh, don't worry. Wait a while, we'll have the same condition with the bakers, too.

THE SAX I'm hep, baby. Yeah, and if it keeps comin' in like this, the candlestick makers, too. (*Gleefully*) Everybody will be high!

SARAH Candles I'm not worried. Once a year, on Chanukah, I can afford it.

THE SAX Wail, mamala. All of 'em: doctors, lawyers, Indian chiefs, rich men, poor men, beggar men, thieves! Uptown! Downtown. All around the high town. (*He sings*) "We'll have Manhattan, the Bronx, and Staten Island, too."
(*A short blast on his saxophone.* SARAH *smiles*)

SARAH That's right. Once it begins, it's like the measles. But not my butcher on Houston. Now there's a real human person. A profit he makes, but a robber he's not. Such a nice man. Eleven years, he never disappointed me. Special he orders a pullet for me every week. Friday I make chicken paprikash. You ever try it?

THE SAX No.

SARAH Oh, it's very good. Next to knish, Herbie's favorite. A little chopped onion with wine just right. Mushrooms and boullion and a lot of sour cream. (THE SAX *stares at her*) So it's not so kosher, but once in a while, enjoy you gotta. Right? (THE SAX *nods*) Then the paprika. You got to brown the onions just right, though. And you got to be careful to get a good pullet. That's the main thing. One with a fat breast. (*She fishes in her shopping bag*) Look, let me show you. (*She takes out a chicken wrapped in brown wax paper, and unwraps it.* THE SAX *seems hypnotized by her. She holds the chicken up to him, feeling the breast*) Look. Look at that. That's a chicken for paprikash. Meat all over. (*She holds up one of the legs*) Look at that. Did you ever see something like that? Go ahead, feel it. (THE SAX *hesitates*) Go on. It won't bite you. (THE SAX *takes the chicken's head and opens and closes the beak, just to make sure. Convinced, but not completely, he touches the breast, tentatively. Then he wipes his fingers on his trousers, with a sickly smile*) Did you ever feel something like that?

THE SAX (*Shaking his head*) Uh uh.

SARAH   Such a nice man. Eleven years and he never forgets to order for me special. (*The chicken lies in her lap*) Oh, boy, you should see my Herbie eat. Every Friday night at least two hours at the table, with laughing and joking and yelling at me because I never had enough sour cream. Now he lives on Long Island in a fancy house with his wife and two children and I hardly ever see him any more. Aw, it's all right. It's good he should have a life of his own. You got to let them go. That's right. So proud of him. A regular big shot with an office on Madison Avenue and a secretary and a little Italian car what looks like a perculator. So it won't kill me to eat alone. It's funny, I got the habit so long, I can't stop. Friday night; paprikash. Yes, you gotta let them go. (*She stares for a moment, absently, into space, then checks herself and wistfully wraps the chicken up once more and replaces it in her shopping bag. She looks up and sees* THE SAX *watching her*) Are you still living at home?

THE SAX (*Shaking his head*) Uh uh.

SARAH Oh, then your mama feels the same thing, believe me. Do her a favor, will you? See her as much as you can. Don't be a stay-away son.

THE SAX (*Laughing*) Oh, oh, baby, you too much. You know that? You the cream of the crop, the pick of the pack, the best of the brood. Wail, mamala!

SARAH So what did I say that was so funny?

THE SAX Ize a motherless child.

SARAH (*Shocked*) You got no mother?

THE SAX Daz right, honey chile.

SARAH And no family?

THE SAX 'Course I got family. Man, you should see all the kin I got in New York State Orphanage, and the monkey ward in Bellevue. And, man, have I got family in Lexington! They all *love* me there. 'Course we don't have no chicken paprikashala on Friday night, but we

65

make out. Man, have I got family! I told ya! I am the embryo of the universe. I am the amoeba and before that, water and before that, the idea. I am ananda. I am aksa. Family? I got 'em on One hundred and Twenty-sixth Street and Lex. I got 'em on Mulberry and Mott. I got 'em on Eighty-second, and Amsterdam, Canal, Avenue C and third, Coney, One hundred and Eighty-fourth, the Bronx, Twentieth and Eighth, Forty-second. I got 'em on the Third Avenue El, on the A, the D, the E train, the Canarsie Line. I got 'em on Fulton Street, Broome, Church, De Kalb Avenue. (*A short honk on his saxophone*) I got 'em!

SARAH   But you really don't have any relatives of your own?

THE SAX   (*Defiantly*)   Sure! Sure I do!

SARAH   Who?

THE SAX   (*Thinks a moment, then grins*)   Well, I got a few Uncle Toms.

SARAH   Yeah? You see them often?

THE SAX   Not much. They mostly stay down south.

SARAH   Oh, that's a shame.

THE SAX   That's what I say. You see . . . (*He catches himself*) Hey, baby, look, are you puttin' me on?

SARAH   I'm not putting nothing on you. It's nice you have some uncles. How come they all have the same name?

66

THE SAX (*Agitated*) Er . . . look, mamala, what say we drop it, huh? I was just jazzin' ya.

SARAH Jazzing?

THE SAX Yeah, you know. Like jokin' . . . kiddin'.

SARAH Kidding?

THE SAX Uh huh.

SARAH There's no uncles?

THE SAX Uh uh.

SARAH You got nobody?

THE SAX Uh uh.

SARAH (*Shaking her head*) He's got nobody, and he kids. Some joke. Pardon me if I shouldn't laugh.

THE SAX I don't need anybody, see? I swing. I mean like you got barnacles hangin' on ya, how ya gonna make it to Yucatán on a peyotle pilgrimage, when you get the twitch. I mean, how you gonna make the happenin's, dig?

SARAH That's what people are to you; barnacles?

THE SAX Me and Nelson Eddy, baby, we the vagabond kings. I don't need anybody. I don't need diddly. (*He caresses his saxophone*) I got my man here, and we wail.

67

(*Speaks into the opening*) Right? (*A honk in response to his question*) See? He understands me. I mean, when I get my hot breath goin' through his guts, there's nothin', nothin' else. Up, down, and around and around the sound. And it's me and him and we's blowin' drifts off Everest. We's lookin' down at the stars. We's out-Gabin' Gabriel. We *swing!*

SARAH   You swing, ha?

THE SAX   Yeah, baby.

SARAH   So can it take your temperature when you're sick?

THE SAX   Oh, man . . .

SARAH   Well can it? Does it know how to make a mustard plaster or chicken soup or call on the telephone for some medicine in case, God forbid, you should need some medicine? So what's the matter with people?

THE SAX (*Turning away from her*) People, steeple people, lethal people, creeple people, feeple, deeple, neeple, gleeple, seeple, people. Drags . . . drags! Phony . . . phony . . . phony! (*In his British accent*) Extremely distasteful.

SARAH   Who else you got?

THE SAX   Me. Me and my man! And sound, baby. You dig? You know what that is, mama? It's mama. It's cool and sweet and clean. It's mine and my man's. It's happy and sad and it don't need nobody but me and him to make it that way. Nobody! And it don't make pain for nobody. And the fuzz can't take it. And the Bible slappers can't take it. We make it, and nobody can take it. And my man's always there when it's cold and there's no horse, when it's night and rainy and there's no junk. He's always there and he's straight and true and he's enough. He's orgone, baby. You understand?

SARAH No.

THE SAX (*Disgusted*) Yeah, well it figures.

SARAH Listen, I know what you're talking about, but it doesn't mean I have to understand.

THE SAX Man, she's puttin' me on again.

SARAH You're a grown man and you don't even know a little about living.

THE SAX (*Laughs*) I don't know. (*Laughs*) Oh, man, you too much. (*He speaks into the opening of the saxophone*) Wembly to flight leader. Wembly to . . .

SARAH No, you don't. And don't play another game on me. It won't help you.

THE SAX I don't need help. You deaf or somethin'?

SARAH I'm not deaf and you're wrong. First you say you got family all over in Coney Island and Canarsie and the

Bronx, and then you say you don't need anybody. People are barnacles? Listen, everybody should be so lucky and have a few. You think they're not important, you're crazy. You think a saxingphone is enough, you're crazy. Nothing takes the place. Heartbreak it can give you, believe me. I know. When Herbie was young, popular he wasn't. He was naturally shy and the pimples didn't help him, neither. So he didn't go around much with the other kids. Movies and the library. That was my Herbie. He was an old man at fifteen. And I couldn't do anything. Heartbreak, believe me. I know. Then, he went in with the army. Everything changed. He was with people all the time. You should read some of the letters I got from him. What a change. You don't even know a little about living if you think that thing (*She indicates the saxophone*) can take the place of a human person.

THE SAX   Cut out, baby. Try the ASPCA.

SARAH   He makes wisecracks, yet. He thinks it's funny.

THE SAX (*Picks up his imaginary phone and dials*)   Hello, Frankenstein laboratories? Lemme talk to Frank. Hello, Frankie, baby? Say, man, I want you to send over one of them human persons you been turnin' out there. I don't care. Any shape. Any color. You pick it out. Surprise me. Yeah. (*Then, looking directly at* SARAH *as he speaks into the phone*) Oh, say, Frankie, baby, one thing. Would you check it out and make sure it doesn't have any greed? That's right. Also, deceit, and hate, and paranoia, and violence and ignorance. Would you?

You don't *have* any without them things? Oh, that's a drag. Yeah, I understand. Ok. Say hello to all the boys in the lab. Keep in touch, hear? (*He hangs up, then grins at* SARAH) He don't have none without. How about that?

SARAH (*Smiling. She gets the point*) That's not a person you're asking for. It's a saint. There's none around here, believe me. Are you digging? They live some other place.

THE SAX (*Angrily*) Well I don't!

SARAH I don't either. So how come everybody's got to be a saint for you to like them?

THE SAX They don't have to be *nothin'!* I just want them to leave me alone! I want *you* to leave me alone. Is you diggin' *me?*

SARAH All right. I'll leave you alone. Don't get nervous. Two people say a few words to each other, nobody should have to get nervous.

THE SAX *Grand!*

SARAH But a little quiet argument never hurt anybody. You want I should change benches?

THE SAX (*His eyeballs rolled back in his forehead*) It don't matter. Ize just yogaed you out of my fore-con-sciousness. My Karma body has gobbled your identity and the Bodhisattvas are dancin' ring around the rosy

71

all fall down around your ghost. You have been osmotized into my Nirvana!

SARAH   Is that good?

THE SAX   It's better than pizza!

SARAH   That's nice. (*She leans back, looking up into the trees*) Such nice birds. It reminds me sometimes on Sundays, before my husband Jules . . . God rest his sweet soul, . . . before he went to rest, he would take me and Herbie down to the Battery. To the old Aquarium.

THE SAX   Solarium, Planetarium, Sanitarium.

SARAH   Such a nice park there. And such fishes you could see there. Sharks and octopuses. You know, with a hundred arms?

THE SAX   Are you bothered by falling hair, falling gamma particles?

SARAH   Such a fish that one is. There was a little delicatessen near the park. I remember it had kosher frankfurters.

THE SAX   It's regulation. We wrap you up in this wet sheet for two weeks, and you'll be well again.

SARAH   So wonderful. So crispy. They snap when you bite them.

THE SAX Those giant insects you're seeing are part of the illusionary visiopsychic side effects caused by the reduction of dosages during your withdrawal.

SARAH Between them, they could eat half a dozen.

THE SAX (*His Welfare voice*) Do you consider yourself in the below-average income bracket?

SARAH Not to mention a coupl'a cream sodas apiece. Once, even, we took the ferry to the Statue of Liberty.

THE SAX (*His pushcart vender voice*) Lady, a whatsa matta you? Please no toucha da figs. Nonchu see they soft?

SARAH Jules was very proud. A very patriotic man, he was. He cried. We went up inside the torch and he cried.

THE SAX (*His voice*) Like, man, we gonna blow. We gonna wail. And everybody's gonna get high and juiced out'a his gourd! And we gonna shake *up* some cement! There's gonna be happenin's, baby, *happenin's!*

SARAH That was a day I'll never forget. And Herbie, he wasn't ashamed to see his father cry. He was proud. Proud like him.

THE SAX It's wide, man, wide. And nobody's closin' any doors. We's goin' out on the rooftops to watch the mushroom grow.

SARAH   And then, that night, cocoa and a strudel before bed and nobody could talk. All sitting in the kitchen and nobody talking.

THE SAX (*Quietly*)   Yeah, man, happenin's like you never dug before. We'll all get high and juiced to watch.

SARAH   Such a day that was.

THE SAX   And . . . and we'll all have cocoa and strudel . . .

SARAH   Such a day.

THE SAX   Yeah.

SARAH (*A long moment of silence as they move back into their respective thoughts.* SARAH *shakes her head, wistfully*)   It seems like everything happens yesterday, last week, last year. Such a thief is time, you know? A regular robber.

THE SAX (*Not looking at her, touched by the note of quiet sadness they have both created*)   Yeah, well it's like when you take a clock, dig? And you turn it. And then you got . . . well . . . you know . . . like it's turnin' backwards like. And that means like . . . oh, man, you know. Like that.

SARAH (*Nodding*)   That's so true.
(*There is another moment of silence.* THE SAX *unfolds a small, three-sided sun reflector of the type that is held under the chin. He holds it under his*

74

chin. SARAH *stares incredulously, then begins laughing softly*)

THE SAX   Wazza matter? Wazza matter with you?

SARAH (*Trying to control her laughter*)   Pardon . . . pardon my laughing, but it seems a little ridiculous you should be wanting a tan.

THE SAX   That's how much you know. It happens I've become rather pale with too much indoor living. If them office cats in Rockefeller Center can do this, so can I. You got any objections?

SARAH   No, no. Why should I object? (*Giggling*) You do what you want. You wanna look crazy, go ahead. It's your life.
(*Her giggle gets away from her.* THE SAX *does not respond. He sits defiantly, his face in the reflector. The sound of* SARAH's *infectious laughter begins to reach him, though. He knows she's onto his ruse. His face begins to break into a smirk. He tries to control it. He has to turn away from her to hide it. Then, as* SARAH's *laughter continues,* THE SAX *begins to giggle as well. His giggle builds until he is laughing along with her.* SARAH *is laughing so much, there are tears in her eyes.* THE SAX, *unable to hold it any longer, surrenders himself to his laughter, joining with her*)

THE SAX (*Throwing the reflector into the air*)   Wee oo, baby, you too much. Wail, chick, *wail!*

(*Their laughter joins again and finally subsides. From his tote bag, he takes one of those novelty arrows that clip to and appear to pass through the head*)

SARAH (*Wiping her eyes and blowing her nose*)   Excuse, excuse me. Oh, my goodness. Oh, you're a bad boy to do such a thing to me.
(THE SAX *grins*)

THE SAX (*Innocently*)   Who me? I didn't do nothin'. (*He turns to* SARAH *who, just about controlling her laughter, sees* THE SAX *with the arrow and bursts out once more.* THE SAX *joins her. He stamps his feet, he jumps up and down on the bench, he honks his saxophone, he makes it laugh*) Wail, baby!
(*Their laughter subsides once more. He takes the arrow off, and replaces it in the bag*)

SARAH (*Catching her breath*)   Oh, you're such a bad boy.

THE SAX (*Shaking his finger at her*)   And you is such a bad girl.
(*He chuckles, then all quiets to silence. Both become lost in their own thoughts. There is no sound except for the birds in the trees above them*)

SARAH (*Blows her nose again, then looks at* THE SAX *who has resumed shining his saxophone. She seems to be sizing him up for something*)   Listen, tomorrow night, you got a big date or something?

THE SAX   Uh uh.

SARAH   Well, it's only a suggestion and you shouldn't feel insulted and if you say no I won't be insulted either and believe me, it has nothing to do with no shoes.

THE SAX   What's on your mind, mamala?

SARAH   Well, as I said, you shouldn't be insulted. It's not charity. It's an invitation. An invitation between two people. (THE SAX *looks at her, curiously*) You wanna come tomorrow night for chicken paprikash?

THE SAX   Send that one again?

SARAH   You wanna come eat chicken with me tomorrow night?

THE SAX (*Suddenly feeling betrayed*)   Are you kiddin'?

SARAH   What's to kid? It's a simple question.

THE SAX   Look, when I need soup I'll go to Welfare.

SARAH   What's the matter you didn't hear I said an invitation, not charity?

THE SAX   Yeah, how's come you're invitin' *me*?

SARAH   Well . . . I just . . . thought maybe . . .
    (*She is at a loss to explain*)

THE SAX (*Angrier*)   How *come*?

SARAH   I just thought you would like to have a home meal, that's all. So what is it a crime?

THE SAX   Listen, baby. I don't want your three bucks. And I don't want your chicken. Man, you comin' off with some bad jazz. I don't *want* it, hear?

SARAH   All right! So call the police and have me arrested for asking!

THE SAX   Don't come off with that jive to me.

SARAH   All *right!* Finish it, would you? (*Silence*) I don't know what's the matter. Everytime I open my mouth I gotta make an apology?

THE SAX   You is goin' back in my Karma body. I should'a never left you out.

SARAH   So I'm back.

THE SAX   (*Concentrating, his eyes closed*) Yeah, yeah. That's it. Swingin'. Now! Now, you know what you are?

SARAH   What?

THE SAX   Obliterated!

SARAH   Wonderful. I hope you'll be very happy. (*Silence*) I never saw such a touchy person. You can't say a word without becoming an enemy. (*She leans toward him*)

78

Listen, I'm *no* enemy. Sometimes I make mistakes, like with the three dollars, but an enemy, I'm not.

THE SAX (*Ignoring her*)   You is air, chick. Less than that: a vacuum totalis!

SARAH   I know what's the matter. You think I don't understand? What a foolish boy. You think I raised a boy your age without understanding even a little? You wanna be independent because it's a crazy world and it scares you. And it's a dragging.

THE SAX (*Still turned away from her*)   Yeah, baby, you got all the answers.

SARAH   Not all. Maybe a few. Who's got all of them? Only those saints you're asking for. Take a little advice, don't be afraid.

THE SAX   Afraid? Me? Do I look afraid?

SARAH   You should pardon my honesty, yes.

THE SAX   Oh, man . . .

SARAH   Well you do. What's the matter with some friendliness? You know what? I think you got some kind of syndrome.

THE SAX (*Sarcastically, a saccharine smile*)   You don't say?

79

SARAH That's right. The health section of the paper it says people that act like you, they got syndromes. I don't know exactly what it means, but I think you got one.

THE SAX Thanks for the info.

SARAH You're welcome, I'm sure. I think that's what Herbie had before he went in with the army. And you know what's the cure?

THE SAX (*His Freud accent*) No. Tell me, Doctor Noodle-neck.

SARAH Nodelman.

THE SAX Oh, ja.

SARAH People.

THE SAX Oh, ja?

SARAH That's right. Talking and laughing and working with them.

THE SAX Vorking?

SARAH What's the matter, that's not part of living? I'm sure you could get a good job playing your saxingphone somewhere.

THE SAX A good job, like Herbie?

SARAH   That's right.

THE SAX   Maybe even get a pair of shoes?

SARAH   Why not? And a suit maybe.

THE SAX   And a house on Long Island?

SARAH   Sure. And then a wife and children and you got somebody.

THE SAX   And a little Italian car. (*His* SARAH *accent*) Vat looks like a perculator?
(*He is angry and there is a sharp, unfriendly, edge to his sarcasm now*)

SARAH   It's possible. You could have anything you wanted if you wasn't afraid to take a chance. You see, there it comes back to being afraid.

THE SAX   (*His anger mounting*)   What else could I have, mamala?

SARAH   Anything. Maybe a little bungalow on the beach.

THE SAX   Yeah?

SARAH   And a rowboat to go fishing.

THE SAX   Uh huh.

SARAH   And Book-of-the-Month Club.

THE SAX   Oh, my, *that's* a good one.

SARAH   One of those credit cards. Wouldn't that be nice?

THE SAX   Lovely.

SARAH   Listen, what am I talking about. Those are all just *things*. Most of all is, you could have a family and that would be somebody.

THE SAX   (*Screams. He can no longer stand it*)   Aggggggh! And how about an ocarina? Could I have one of them, *too?*

SARAH   (*Surprised at his anger*)   What's the matter?

THE SAX   I don't *want!* *That's* what's the matter. I hate them things you been rattlin' your trap about. I don't want clean shirts, or a house, or a car, or a bungalow on the beach. I don't want no family! I don't want to belong to nobody and nothin'. You dig? Is that plain? I hate them. And I hate the cats that got 'em. And I hates the cats that talk about 'em. 'Cause you know what it means? Nothin'! Minus zero! We gonna break, break it all up and it don't matter who's got what and who's got who. We gonna have a helluva time when it goes, mamala! An' that's why I hate it. I can't wait. I wanna start right now. I wanna start breakin' it up right now! Yeah! Burn it up, break it up, shake it up! Yeah! (*He picks up his saxophone and begins to play. The music is unlike any we have heard before. It is wild, destructive, cacophonic, dissonant. It has the scream of revolt, destruction, chaos, in it. It breaks all the rules of harmony and melody. Yet, in its wildness, there is a frightening beauty about it. It expresses the rhythm of the age. It is formless, yet with a form and validity of its own. It is relentless, clear in its meaning, uncompromising in its message.* SARAH *watches, spellbound and frightened by it.* THE SAX *sweats. He circles* SARAH, *blasting her with the sounds of his protest. The notes are like hammer blows against her. The piece ends in a final, maddening shout chorus, a crescendo of dissonance.* THE SAX, *sweating, breathless, continues where the saxophone left off)* You get on the train and go out to Long Island and take *Herbie's* temperature! Herbie, with his office and his car. You take *him* home for paprikashala, buy *him* a pair of sneakers. Take *him* to the Statue of Liberty! You lonely? Go to your Herbie, but for Chris' sakes leave me *alone!*

(He goes back to the saxophone. This time the music is even more awesome than before. It is the ultimate in his expression of anger and fear. He ends his statement by blowing the last note in SARAH's *face. He sits back on the bench, turned away from her, breathing hard.* SARAH *looks at him for a moment, then wipes the tears from her eyes. She puts her crocheting in her shopping bag, and is about to get up and leave when she checks herself. Something is still undone, unsaid. She turns to* THE SAX *and begins speaking quietly)*

SARAH   I'm sorry you feel that way. I'll leave you alone. What a world. Where's the sense of it? Here I am and I can't even converse with a fellow human person. I feel like a worthless nothing. Everything's changing and

83

something's wrong. I don't know what, but I know it's wrong when a thing like this can happen.

THE SAX (*Turning away from her*) Oh, man . . .

SARAH All right. A minute, then I'll go. First I wanna tell you something. You know you were talking about people being phonies? Well maybe that's what's wrong. Maybe it's *me*. I'm making a confession. I'm a phony. (THE SAX *turns toward her*) I can't help it. Listen. My Herbie don't live on Long Island in a nice home with a nice family. And I can't take his temperature and buy him sneakers. You see, my Herbie don't live at all. He died in Korea, in Nineteen Fifty-one. (*There is a long silence.* THE SAX *lets out a stream of air, not quite a whistle*) So I'm a phony liar. I'm sorry. (*Silence*) They didn't even find anything, not even a dog tag or a shoe lace. It's funny how things happen. One second, there's a Herbie in the world, the next, there's not. It's a gyp, that's what it is. A buddy came to see me. It happened in a place by the name of K-Eleven. What kind of place is that for a nice bar-mizvahed Jewish boy to die in? What kind of a country is that with places with names such as that? So I'm making up a big story. And I'm a phony. Still, it's not such a *big* lie. He was a good boy. He would have had all those things. I'm sure of it. So it's an old lady making up stories. An old, foolish, ridiculous lady who can't pass Friday night without making paprikash and looking at an empty chair. You're right to get mad. I thought since you didn't have nobody and me neither . . . I thought . . . Well it's done. (THE SAX *has been staring at her intently during this speech. She looks at* THE SAX) That's my confession. I'm sorry I lied to you. (*There is a long silence. Slowly,* THE SAX *picks up his saxophone and begins to play. The music is a sad jazz and into it is woven "Home on the Range," along with old Hebraic melodies. These are notes of compassion and sorrow, not anger now. This music is balm. It works outward, caressing, giving, soft and understanding in* SARAH's *terms.* SARAH *smiles as she recognizes the melodies. This is Herbie's theme, a farewell, an echo for* SARAH *to have. In it we can hear an ocarina playing. It is the only gesture, the only method of compassion.* THE SAX *knows how to make. He ends on a long, plaintive note. There are tears in the corners of his eyes.* SARAH *nods, smiling. She has understood. She has accepted. She speaks quietly, choked*) Thank you. Thank you, so much.

(THE SAX, *embarrassed, moves to leave*)

THE SAX   Well . . . like . . . er. I'll see you, baby. I gotta . . . Well, I gotta go meet the Wolf Man, dig?

SARAH (*Quietly*)   I dig.

THE SAX   Ok?

SARAH   Ok.

THE SAX   Take care, hear!

SARAH   You too. (THE SAX *crosses to stage left and exits, playing a bouncy cool jazz.* SARAH *sits for a moment, composing herself. She blows her nose and smiles at*

85

the birds in the trees above her. She shakes her head and looks after THE SAX) The Wolf Man! Such a kidder. (*She chuckles to herself*) And he calls me a *baby*. At my age!

> (*She laughs again, then takes everything in; the park, the trees. She sighs deeply, and continues her crocheting*)

Curtain